The **DEFINITIVE GUIDE** to **BEAR BAITING IN ALASKA**

(LESSONS-LEARNED THE HARD WAY SO YOU DON'T HAVE TO)

D1521265

By
D. Patrick

All photos by author unless otherwise noted
Illustrations by Krystal Moulton
Design and Layout by Elena Reznikova

Dedication

To all those who have dedicated their lives towards the
protection and oversight of our public lands, ensuring the
sustainability of Alaska's natural resources for past,
present and future generations to enjoy!

Special thanks to my wife, Bowe, for always being a
better sport than even she would have imagined, and to
my sons for all the free labor and hundreds of hours in
the stands enjoying each other's company...
in silence!

Acknowledgments

I WOULD LIKE TO THANK the many folks who were so often willing to share their knowledge and lifelong experience of bear hunting with me since my family and I arrived in Alaska over a decade ago. Each person had some unique skill set, knowledge base or first-hand insight (BS or not) that shaped the way my sons and I hunt bears today.

Special thanks to the following individuals, though I apologize in advance for leaving folks out, predominantly due to "old timers" rather than intentional oversight:

Lon Rake for giving up a "toad" of a bear so that my middle son could experience the taking of our family's first bear...the bear that started it all. Still the best rug in the house;

Dave Kueber who was (and is) a professional BS'r, but rallied from his "sick bed" to share the finer points of skinning out a bear, in the dark!;

Bill Comer for being even a bigger BS'r than Kueber, but always willing to scale a cliffside or walk a river bed while looking for that bear that we were POSITIVE we hit...but didn't. Thanks for sharing in another family first, as you played a critical role in the taking of my youngest son's first bear, which really launched our obsession with all things associated with bear baiting;

Chris Farmer for being the "Macgyver" of the crew and ALWAYS willing to carry a load or finagle a "fix" when it seemed none existed. I think our trailer would still be on the mountain without your jury-rigging. And yes, that "boar" was a "sow" (sorry)—still a beautiful bear!;

Steve Weeks for always being "on call" to lend a hand, or share in the search party that ultimately found the bear we weren't looking for; and lastly

Trooper Tony Beck for his willingness to readily assist in answering questions or clarifying the finer points of those ever-changing regulations. I guess I should have asked more questions!

DISCLAIMER: Any regulatory information noted in this book is intended to provide the reader with a general summary of the regulations as outlined in the 2018-2019 version of the Alaska Hunting Regulations, and was accurate at the time of publication. Please ensure you consult the most current version of the regulations appropriate to the regulatory year you are hunting in, prior to applying this information specifically to your bear baiting operation(s). For direct-source information, consult Title 5 of the Alaska Administrative Code and Title 16 of Alaska Statutes for additional specificity.

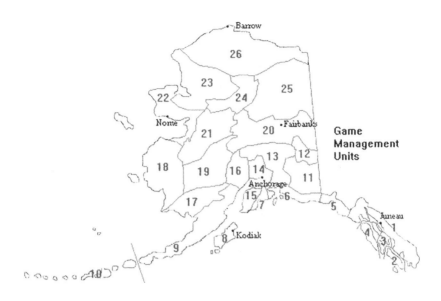

ALASKA ENCOMPASSES OVER 663,000 SQUARE MILES, or about 375,000,000 acres of land totaling 1/5 the size of the entire lower 48. In certain parts of Alaska, temperatures range from over 100 degrees F in the summer to less than -60 degrees F in the dark of winter. As such, Alaska is home to over 30,000 brown/grizzly bears (representing 98% of all brown/grizzly bears in the U.S. and 70% of all brown/grizzly bears on the continent). In addition, Alaska is home to over 100,000 black bears (representing 33% of all black bears in the U.S. and 17% of all black bears on the continent).

It's no wonder that when you speak with fellow bear baiters across the state, they have varied experiences (and opinions) on the best ways to bait bears in Alaska. These same factors also contribute towards individual differences in size, color, and type of bears within different geographic regions of the state, as well as subsets within those regions. It's important to keep this in mind as you read through this book and adapt, as necessary, any general information as it pertains to your particular region(s) within the Last Frontier.

of Alaska

INTRODUCTION

THOUGH TITLED THE "DEFINITIVE" GUIDE to bear baiting in Alaska, this book is not intended to replace or circumvent any part of the Alaska Hunting Regulations. It is your responsibility as both an ethical hunter and conservationist, to familiarize yourself with all applicable regulations that may pertain to the specific **Game Management Unit (GMU)** or units in which you plan to hunt. Changes to these regulations may occur from season to season, so make sure you're using the most current edition before setting up your bait station(s).

Copies of the regulations are free of charge and can be obtained through your local Alaska Department of Fish and Game (ADF&G), local State Trooper's Office, or at various outdoor retail stores, as well as online at www.adfg.alaska.gov. If you have questions related to any portion of these regulations, never hesitate to contact your nearest ADF&G office or local State Wildlife Trooper for assistance. These folks are a phenomenal resource and are always willing to help—but please, be respectful of their time and do your homework first. Then if you still have questions, call or stop by to address specific questions or concerns. Remember, these folks are responsible for the management of tens of thousands of acres and millions of dollars in natural resources, so their time is precious.

In the end, the only one responsible for ensuring compliance with the regulations is you. Once you've set your stand, there is no room for excuses on why you failed to comply with any number of requirements. Believe me...I know from first-hand experience. :)

So, be good, be smart and be safe...you are about to embark on one of the funnest (yes—that's a word) hunting experiences there is. Remember to enjoy every moment—they won't all be fun, but they will be memorable.

Good luck and enjoy!

Contents

The **DEFINITIVE GUIDE** to **BEAR BAITING IN ALASKA**

(LESSONS-LEARNED THE HARD WAY SO YOU DON'T HAVE TO)

In a civilized and cultivated country wild animals only continue to exist at all when preserved by sportsmen. The excellent people who protest against all hunting, and consider sportsmen as enemies of wild life, are ignorant of the fact that in reality the genuine sportsman is by all odds the most important factor in keeping the larger and more valuable wild creatures from total extermination.

—Theodore Roosevelt

PART 1. BAITING VS. SPOT-AND-STALK

THERE ARE VARYING OPINIONS ON the topic of baiting bears versus spot-and-stalk. To some, bear baiting is considered unethical or unsporting while to others, it is considered a way to enhance the selection process. Others view it as merely an alternative way to hunt. In the end, it is simply about personal preference. This book is not intended to convert, convince or defend the legitimacy of baiting bears to those who are opposed to this technique. It is simply written as a resource for those wishing to educate themselves (whether as a 1st-time bear hunter or seasoned veteran) on this somewhat unique and always exciting process.

Many people over the years have asked why people would bait bears rather than simply using spot-and-stalk techniques. For those who may be unfamiliar with the term, spot-and-stalk simply refers to spending time "glassing" (using optics such as binoculars, or spotting scopes) to survey hillsides and forested areas for bears, and then once spotted, heading out on foot or machine in pursuit of the animal.

There are many reasons why bear baiting is both accepted and encouraged by game management officials, but the overarching reason focuses on *enhanced species selection*. So what is meant by this?

If you have ever been walking through the woods or hiking along a hillside and had the opportunity to encounter a bear in its natural environment, you can relate to the adrenaline-filled moment. Depending on how far away and how fleeting the encounter all contribute towards the experience. As an avid bear hunter over many years, the following unscientific observations typically apply to unplanned bear sightings in thick cover or spotted on distant hillsides:

1. Bears typically appear to look bigger than they actually are.
2. Bears typically appear to be male (unless they are with cubs).
3. Bears typically appear to be closer than they actually are.

Adding to this predisposed mindset, nearly half of all televised outdoor hunting shows focused on hunting both black and brown bears (and I have watched hundreds) typically cast the fallen bear as "he" even though it is distinctly female from my perch on the couch. More egregious errors come in the way of reported measurements with "professional" hunters shooting a black bear that would conservatively "square" (we'll discuss how to measure a bear later on) at a respectable 6 feet, only to hear the closing commentary refer to this 9-foot bear? I know it makes for more exciting television, but come on folks!

So…how does baiting help? Here are a few ways:

1. *Having a game camera at your bait site provides a visual history of not only what bears are frequenting your site, but also provides a timeline of what bears typically arrive and when.*

Having this information will help you plan what time you want to sit in your stand as well as providing you with an idea of what bears you have to choose from. For example, if you know you have a nice 6 foot black bear coming into your stand each night, and while your waiting, a decent 5½ ft black bear arrives—you now can make an educated decision on whether you want to take the bear in your sights or wait, knowing there is a better-than-average chance that a bigger bear will be arriving soon. The bait site creates a repeat destination for bears, which in turn, provides you with an ideal location to place a camera to provide information in your absence.

2. *Bears are notoriously hard to judge when it comes to size. Depending on what you use to hold your bait (we'll discuss setting up your site later on), such as plastic barrels, steel drums, etc., you will provide yourself with a readily known reference point or measurement gauge to help you determine the size of the bears frequenting your bait site.*

For example, if you use a standard 55-gallon drum (standing upright) to hold your bait, your drum is typically 34 inches tall. Bears with a shoulder height of around 36" while standing on all fours, will typically square out at 6 feet or bigger. So using hunter's math, if you want to shoot a bear that is approximately 6 feet or bigger, his shoulders should be at or above the top of your barrel. In addition, I typically paint a line (or 2) on the tree the barrel is chained to, clearly marking a 3ft and 6ft mark for easy reference. If you use the same type barrel laying on its side (measuring approx 24" high), then in order to shoot a 6ft bear, his shoulders would have to be approx 1 ft above the height of the barrel while on all fours.

The point is, whatever you use (stake in the ground, old tree limb set at a known height (aka: limbo pole), etc.), as long as you have a known measurement that you can use to compare to the height of your bear, you'll be just fine. Though I'm using 6ft as a reference point above, there is nothing wrong with shooting a smaller bear (e.g. 5–5½ ft) as the "standard" size bear may vary with the GMU you're in. The choice is up to you, and you alone. A quick rule of thumb if needed is 'if you're not sure or have to convince yourself that's the bear you want—you might want to pass and wait for a better opportunity.'

3. *Judging the sex of a bear. Much like judging the size of a bear, determining if the bear you are looking at is male (boar) or female (sow) can be difficult at times. Add the challenge of looking through alders, underbrush and distance, and your ability to determine the sex of a bear can be almost impossible.*

Though there is nothing that requires a hunter to take only boars, it is generally agreed upon that for conservation purposes, it is always better to take the male of the species to ensure a sustainable population. Having a bait site allows you time and (as previously indicated) the ability to set up game cameras to examine bears at your leisure and aid in sex identification. Having photos of your bears will allow you to take a closer look and/or ask other hunters their opinion if you are unsure. Some male characteristics to look for in identifying boars from sows include:

a. **Head and neck:** Mature males have rounded heads and thicker necks (meaning their neck and head are seemingly one), while females and young males have narrower faces and thinner necks. In addition, mature males will have a furrow or crease running down the middle of their foreheads.

b. **Ears:** Adult males have what appear to be smaller ears closer on their heads, while females and young bears have what appear to be larger ears closer together (think Mickey Mouse). The reason for this is due to the fact that a bear's ears stop growing after the first year but their heads continue growing—particularly in width.

c. **Nose:** Male bears tend to have shorter, more "blocky" noses while females and young bears have longer/narrower noses (like a German Shepherd).

d. **Urination:** Male bears urinate towards the front while females urinate towards the back.

e. **Behavior:** Male bears will approach your bait site more confidently and deliberately. Sows (especially with cubs) or younger bears will approach more cautiously, and will typically arrive earlier on your bait than a larger male.

Regardless of these differences, it is still sometimes difficult to tell a boar from a sow. So, do your homework—watch bear identification videos, share pictures with other hunters/friends, and observe as many bears as possible, both in person and on camera. Some hunters use tricks, such as "honey pots" to assist in making a more accurate identification. Simply secure a small can or box filled with honey or other strong scent to a tree at a standing height, in a location where the bear would face your stand or blind. When the bear stands up to investigate, you can readily observe the underside of the bear and determine its sex.

There are many other benefits to baiting vs. spot-and-stalk but at this point, you get the picture. Just remember that this is based on personal preference and there's no reason why you can't enjoy both methods if and when the situation permits.

PART 2. GETTING STARTED

STEP 1: Hunting License. First things first—if you're about to go bear hunting, regardless of method, you'll need a hunting license. Alaskan hunters 16 years of age and younger are not required to possess a hunting license (as of this printing). Don't forget to sign your license before heading out.

STEP 2: Online Bear Baiting Clinic (free). Go to the Alaska Department of Fish and Game (ADF&G) web site (**www.adfg.alaska.gov**), hit the "Hunting Tab", then hit the "Hunter Education" sub-tab, and choose the free Online Bear Baiting Clinic. Once you have passed, save and print your certificate.

STEP 3: Harvest Ticket (free). Go to the ADF&G website under "Hunting Tab" and hit "Get your permit/harvest ticket." Follow the steps and ensure you choose the correct harvest ticket for the species and area you will be hunting. For most areas, the "General Season Black Bear" harvest ticket will suffice. This is a free permit to Alaska residents. Please check the current regulations for out-of-state hunter requirements.

STEP 4: Basic Hunter Safety Course (BHSC). Depending on what unit you are hunting, you are required to take a hunter safety course if you are:

a. Born after January 1, 1986, and are 16 years of age or older.

b. If under 16 years of age, you must have either successfully completed the BHSC or be under the direct immediate supervision of a licensed hunter who has taken the course or was born on or before January 1, 1986.

STEP 5: If bowhunting, and born after January 1, 1986, you must have successfully passed an ADF&G approved bowhunter certification course and carry your certification card with you in the field—unless this is not required within the Game Management Unit in which you are hunting.

STEP 6: If using a crossbow, you must have successfully passed an ADF&G approved crossbow certification course and carry your certification card with you in the field—regardless of your birthdate or which GMU you are hunting.

STEP 7: Register your bait station. You must register the location of your bait station (non-guides may register up to 2 stations, guides may register up to 10 stations). You can register your bait station at your nearest ADF&G office, local Wildlife Trooper Office or certain outdoor retail stores in your area. In order to register, you will need to know the location of your bait station prior to registering it. For most Game Management Units (GMU), rough directions (i.e. 1.5 miles north of mile marker xxx off the Richardson Highway) will suffice. Some GMUs require exact latitude/longitude or GPS coordinates—so check the regulations for your specific unit. Once registered, you will receive a *write-in-the-rain* placard to post at your station that identifies who owns the bait station and what other hunters are allowed to use your station. Other hunters may use, put bait at, refill bait or maintain your bait station with your written permission. This written permission must be carried in the field. You may also make your own signs to hang, as long as they clearly identify the site as a "Bear Bait Station" and includes: your Bait Registration number, Hunting License Number, and location. In all likelihood, you will need to replace your sign at some point during the season due to wind/weather/curious bears, etc., so always carry a spare sign in your day pack and a way to secure it to a tree or stand (stapler is my preferred choice). This sign must be posted in the immediate vicinity of your bait station. I typically secure mine to the tree in which my tree stand is placed.

In order to register a bait station, you must:
   a. Be at least 18 years old
   b. Completed a Bear Baiting Clinic
   c. Show proof of license

If others (pre-approved by you) are using your bait station, they can be added to your sign or given written permission from the owner. Due to the amount of work that goes into the establishment of an effective bear baiting station, I am very discerning about who uses my stand—but the choice is up to each individual hunter. Just be aware that you may NOT take money, bartered goods or services from someone using your bait station unless you are a registered guide-outfitter.

Keep in mind—for those of us "chomping at the bit" to get started—Bait Stations may be registered fifteen (15) days prior to the start of your season. However, you cannot place bait at your station until the official opening.

Once the paperwork is complete, it's time to start gathering equipment and supplies. To start, you'll need;

a. A barrel with a short amount of chain (or ratchet straps) to fasten it to a tree—along with a carabiner, double-ended dog chain clip, or some other means to secure it

b. Bait (dog food, used fry grease, old bread, doughnuts, popcorn, etc.)

c. A stand or ground blind

d. A trail camera with extra memory card

e. A way to read your card in the field. You can purchase small card readers that plug directly into your phone. These are available online or at most major outdoor retailers. Note: be sure you buy the correct adapter for your particular phone.

f. Bug repellent (ThermaCell is a lifesaver in the field) and head-net

g. Game bags (never use plastic trash bags as they retain too much heat)

h. A few sharp knives or a Havalon-type replaceable blade model

i. A camera (or phone)

j. A clean tarp for keeping your bear out of the dirt & grass (for field dressing)

k. A small tree and/or bone saw

l. A backpack for carrying your supplies

m. A sturdy plastic sled to assist in hauling your bear out of the heavy brush in which he will inevitably die

PART 3. CHOOSING A LOCATION

THERE ARE LOTS OF OPINIONS as to where you should place a bait station. Let's start with the basics per the regulations.

1. Bait stations must be at least ¼ mile from a publically maintained road, trail or the Alaska Railroad.
2. Bait stations must be at least 1 mile from a: house, school, business, developed recreation facility, campground or permanent dwelling. A permanent dwelling includes seasonally-occupied cabins (including your own). Some areas allow you to have a bait station within one (1) mile from a seasonally-used cabin provided the cabin is on the other side of the river from where the bait site is located, so check the regulations in your specific GMU.
3. You may NOT hunt or kill brown/grizzly bears within one-half mile of a garbage dump or landfill.
4. If you have questions, feel free to contact ADF&G or your nearest Wildlife Trooper.
5. Check the regulations for your specific GMU to ensure other restrictions do not apply to your planned bait site.

Once you have scouted areas and decided on a location, it is important to determine who owns the land on which you plan to establish your bait station. I prefer to bait on state or federal lands (such as State of Alaska or Department of Natural Resources, etc.), though you may hunt on private or Native lands provided you get permission and/or pay for a limited use permit. ADF&G can assist you in determining land ownership before you register and establish your bait station. In addition, there are numerous apps (both free and available for purchase) that can help you determine land ownership via GPS and public records access.

When possible, use a GPS or other applicable app to determine distances, as the ¼ mile and 1-mile requirements are based on "as the crow flies" rather than total distance. I know all too well from first-hand personal experience that even when your 4-wheeler odometer reads 1 ¼ miles, you may be less than ¾ of a mile as the crow flies from the nearest dwelling.

Choose areas that are off the beaten path and require a moderate amount of work to access. Remember—if your site is easily accessible, others will access it, or establish sites nearby. Always scout an area in advance to ensure you are not setting up on top of another hunter. As a rule of thumb, if you are closer than 300-400 yards from another bear bait, you are too close. Be respectful of others and their efforts. Knowingly setting your bait too close to another hunter can—under certain circumstances—be considered as **hunter harassment**, and can draw fines and equipment confiscation from the Troopers. Even in the wilds of Alaska, it seems difficult at times to get away from other hunters, so do your part and other ethical hunters will do theirs.

Physical setting

Though there is no one perfect setting, the following elements can assist in drawing bears to your site:

a. **Choose a location accessible to water.** Whether it's a river, stream, ground spring or mountain run-off location, ready access is key. The longer a bear has to travel from its bedding area to water each day, may affect the timing of your bears' arrival—meaning bears showing up to your site in the darker hours of the Alaskan summer when it's difficult to see your gun sights or bow peephole. Remember, you are not allowed to use lights or other devices that enhance low-light conditions.

b. **Choose a location as far from the road, busy ATV trails or highway noise as possible.** Fortunately for Alaska bear baiters, many of the main highways have very little constant traffic so noise is negligible. If you're in an area with constant vehicle noise, I suggest finding another location.

c. **Choose a location with adequate concealment.** Bears tend to shy away from traveling in open terrain during daylight hours. Natural areas of timber leading to small openings provide good areas for bait stations. Setting your barrel(s) along the edge of a tree line provides the bears a comfortable environment to approach from while providing the hunter with open access for a clean shot.

d. **Avoid setting your bait site in large open areas like fields or beaches**. Bears prefer thick cover such as tall grass, alders or other large trees in order to transit to and from areas.

e. **Facing towards hillsides or sloping terrain leading to water**, such as beaver ponds, provides good terrain for spotting and attracting bears.

f. **Hunter access & egress.** Choose a location you can come and go from that does not intermingle with the natural path the bears will use to access your site. This may take a season or two to figure out if you are establishing a new bait site. Patience and observation are key. Scent killers can be used to spray your boots and clothing to offset this, as bears rely on their exceptional sense of smell to detect danger early.

There are two schools of thought on scent control:

1. Use whatever method desired to mask your scent using various scent control sprays, deodorants and/or wash machine additives; or

2. Make no effort to conceal your scent, and allow the bears to become accustomed to the scent of humans at your particular site. Some hunters actually leave an article of clothing (e.g. old shirt, etc.) to further encourage the bears to become complacent with the scent of humans while feeding.

In the past, I paid little attention to scent control over the years until I started baiting for brown/grizzly bears and learned early on, that they are much more wary of scent than black bears appear to be. With that said, I advocate—at a minimum—a mix of methods and often spray my hunting clothes and boots with scent block, while ignoring the surrounding site and equipment.

Keep in mind that these are simply suggested factors to consider when placing your baits, and for every suggestion, there is a hunter who has a countering opinion and/or example. Be smart and try to think like a bear would. Once bears are habituated to feeding at your bait, I tend to believe many bears (typically black bears) often sense your presence but simply choose to ignore it in lieu of a quick meal.

PART 4. BAIT STATION SET-UP

BLIND VS. TREE STAND. It seems all the rage these days to hunt bears from a ground blind.

The pros for using a ground blind are:
a. They are easy to set-up and take down.
b. They provide more room to stretch out and sit comfortably (depending on what seating you bring).
c. You don't have to worry about donning a harness and hunter safety system to keep you from falling out of a tree.
d. Allows more flexibility while you are trying out new bait locations.

The cons for using a ground blind are:
a. Scent may be harder to conceal at ground level depending on the terrain in which you are hunting.
b. Lower vantage point means longer delays in spotting incoming bears.
c. Provides limited protection when a protective mother bear and her cubs arrive at your bait station and decide to stay a while.
d. Provides even more limited protection when that 9ft grizzly shows up and feels ornery.

In the end, as is everything in this guide, the final choice is up to you. I personally prefer tree stands for various reasons with safety being paramount, coupled with sightline access to a much larger swath of terrain. If you are seeking flexibility while trying out different areas, *climbing stands* provide a reasonable compromise while providing the security and oversight of a traditional tree stand.

Choosing the right stand

This is probably one of the most important equipment decisions you will make over the course of your season as it will ultimately affect the quality of your hunting experience. I have spent countless hours (literally hundreds) sitting in ladder stands, climbing stands, and homemade stands, and have a decidedly strong opinion that bigger is usually better. This, of course, is dependent—as always—on the location (terrain, density of brush, distance from road, etc.). I have spent long all-night "sits" crammed into a supposedly "2-person" ladder stand with my 6'-2" son waiting on brown/grizzly bears to return—realizing that the

stand was realistically designed for one full-size adult and maybe some gear. Granted, the stand cost me less than $100 and was fairly lightweight—which allowed us to position it in a rather remote location. However, the toll a 12+ hour "sit" takes when there is no room to readjust or stretch out, is one worthy of re-evaluating cost and ease of transport.

Whether you hunt alone or with a partner, it is always nice to have room to readjust, access gear, or stand and stretch, whenever possible. I have since purchased a true 2-person ladder stand that has flex mesh seats (much like outdoor patio furniture) that reduces the need for additional bench cushions and back supports.

Adding a tree stand **blind** to your **ladder stand** provides both protection from the elements as well as additional scent control while maximizing the effectiveness of your Thermacell (or other mosquito repellants).

Blind attached to standard ladder stand. Helps with concealment while protecting you from the elements.

My sons enjoy the flexibility of using **climbing stands** as:

1. They can easily be carried to your bait site by a single hunter

2. Can be repositioned in minutes, and;

3. Are fairly comfortable when adjusted properly—as they typically use a sling-type seat

I'm personally not a fan of these stands as they tend not to feel as secure (nor are they) as a traditional ladder stand. In addition, there is no room to secure gear which then requires the addition of tree hooks—which is not a big deal—other than the fact that I like to set up my site once, and be done, rather than re-adjusting every visit.

Another option is **"hang-on" style tree stands**. These are similar to climbing stands but are not readily adjustable since they are secured using a ratchet strap-type arrangement. In addition, you will need to attach some type of climbing steps in order to access your stand.

Installing new hang-on style tree stand in April.
Note metal climbing steps attached to lower portion of tree.

Sighting in bow from newly-installed hang-on style tree stand
just prior to start of spring season.

21

Regardless of what type of commercially supplied stand you choose to use, you should consider the following:

1. Flexibility to hunt alone or with family & friends
2. Seat or bench that flips up to allow for standing shots (bow or gun)
3. Large platform to store gear and/or backpacks
4. Angled backrest for long periods of inactivity
5. Cushioned or flexible seats for long periods of inactivity
6. Overall height of stand (if using ladder stand) to allow for a greater field of view and assist with scent control

Lastly, you may consider building your own stand. This allows you to construct a stand to your own specifications. I know many folks—myself included—who have built wooden stands to accommodate 2-4 persons (or more) at a time. This allows for additional family or friends to participate in the hunt or can provide extra room to film your hunts or merely invite folks for some exciting bear watching.

This stand was built on a slope in steep terrain and could accommodate up to 3 hunters and their gear.

Homemade Platform Stand with camo netting.
Photo courtesy of Bill Comer, Valdez, AK.

Stand Safety

One common factor that all stands share—regardless of design—is the need for some type of hunter safety system. The majority of commercially sold stands come with harness systems, and you should familiarize yourself with how these systems work. There is typically a video disk enclosed with your stand that outlines proper safety methods. If you don't have access to one of these videos, you can either borrow one from someone with a stand (since it's likely stored in their junk drawer in the kitchen) or simply go online and search for tree stand safety videos.

Setting the stand

The distance you set your bait from your stand depends on several factors including the location of available trees, background, and whether I am hunting with a rifle or a bow. There is no hard-and-fast rule for what distance you should use but a general rule of thumb is between 20-30 yards for bow shots and no more than 40-50 yards for rifle shots. Remember, too close and the bears may gain your scent and become nervous. Too far and you risk taking a bad shot—especially in those early or late light hours when many larger bears tend to arrive at your bait.

Important to note:

1. Identify your potential shooting lane in advance and position your stand and barrel(s) accordingly, so as NOT to shoot in the direction of your access trail, adjacent bait stations or any other areas where there is a potential for other people to walk, hike, or motor in your line of fire.

Photo courtesy of Bill Comer, Valdez, AK.

2. Attempt to familiarize yourself, in advance, with the prevailing winds in your chosen location. Morning and evening winds will typically vary due to thermal changes caused by terrain (i.e. mountain slopes) and/ or rivers and streams. Set stand downwind from bait when possible.

Height is also a factor, as the higher you can get (i.e. 20 ft) will assist in masking your scent—especially if you are looking for a close shot. The compromise, of course, is to set a distance for a reasonable rifle shot and then if you choose to hunt with a bow or crossbow—simply bring a strongly scented bait with you in a can or bucket that you can place on the ground within bow shot. The key is to get the bears acclimated to your bait site. Once they become regulars, you can manipulate their behavior through scent and food.

Barrels

There is no one right type of barrel to use while bear baiting. Size and material will both play a factor, depending on how far you have to travel to your site and what types of bears are prevalent in the area.

The most common barrel is a **55-gallon steel drum**—preferably with a top that comes off (though not necessary). The barrel should have a hole (approximately 6-10 inches in diameter) where the bears can reach in to extract food—and may be located in the upper or lower half of the barrel. There are often a few small holes at the bottom of the barrel (see photos) where food can also be shaken out of and/or grease can flow out once poured

Pictured: Basic 55 gal steel drum with removable lid previously used to hold sandblasting material. To cut the round hole, I simply drew a circle with chalk and drilled a small hole (approx 1") in the center of "chalk" circle. Then I used my jig saw (w/steel cutting blade) and repeatedly cut from center hole, out to the chalk lines in a series of triangles. Once cut, I took a hammer and folded the "pie-shaped" pieces up and inside the drum. I drilled additional holes in the back so it could be secured to a tree with chain. Note small half-moon holes in bottom for additional food access and grease drainage.

into the barrel. These drums should also have holes in the back where a chain can be run through and be attached to a tree using a wide range of fasteners, including carabiners, metal dog clips or locking quick links. Swing through your local hardware store to decide what you want to use. Some hunters fasten their drums with adjustable ratchet straps while others use a combination of both. I personally prefer the use of chain over straps as larger bears (especially brown/grizzly bears) will tend to rip through ratchet straps more easily than chain.

If you can't find a drum with a removable top, you can fill it the old fashion way, by simply pouring your food through the front hole. For simpler use, you may choose to cut an opening in the top and screw a cover with a hinge to the top for easy access and faster fills.

Plastic drums are often used as their light weight makes them easier to transport to your site. The downside is that they are obviously not as sturdy as a steel drum, but if you are carrying them for long distances or up steep inclines, you tend to accept this risk over a possible heart attack!

Note: Barrels can be situated vertically or horizontally (or both). See what works best for your terrain and experiment as needed.

Pictured: simple 50 gal plastic barrel I obtained from the local fish hatchery. It has an oval hole on one end for bear access and is secured to the tree at the other end (left side of barrel) by a chain.

Barrel size

In this case, size does matter depending upon how far you must travel to check your site and how often you plan to refill your baits. If you have a bait station close to home, then you can get away with using a smaller barrel that will require frequent refills—depending on bear activity. If you have to travel longer distances to reach your bait site, then a larger barrel (or several barrels) makes sense as you don't want to risk having bears empty your barrels in your absence and move on to another location. A family of bears with cubs in tow can go through 100 lbs of dog food in a matter of days if left to their own devices. Unfortunately, there's not a lot you can do other than to check your baits (and your cameras) regularly until Papa shows up. I have seen some unique barrel designs that include bars welded across the food opening to limit the "pawful" of food that can be scooped out at any one time.

Where to find barrels

I believe in minimizing costs (being cheap) and recycling (being cheap) when it comes to acquiring barrels. Typically barrels can be found at no or low cost depending on where you live. Check out your local dump, landfill, automotive repair shop or service station for used 55-gallon steel oil drums. Barrels can be washed out using simple dish soap or—depending on their original contents—burned clean in the backyard.

Plastic barrels can be purchased at your local Outdoor Stores (Cabelas, Sportsmans Warehouse, etc.) or salvaged from the same locations listed for steel barrels. If you live near a fish hatchery, many hatcheries order aquacide antifungal chemicals for their fish fry which comes in blue plastic 50-gallon drums.

Check with your local car wash for used soap containers. Often their detergent arrives in 20-30 gallon white plastic drums, which can easily be used for bait stations—using 2-3 of these smaller drums serves the same purpose as a larger drum.

To convert a drum (plastic or steel) into a bait barrel, all you need is a drill and a jig saw. For plastic drums, you can often use a knife to cut your food openings—but just remember that it's easier to hunt with all of your fingers, so take your time and be careful.

Placing your barrel

As previously mentioned, secure your barrel to a sturdy tree (or trees) in a location that can be accessed by the bears using moderate to thick cover. Again—the distance from your stand to the barrel will vary depending on whether you are hunting with a gun, bow, or some other type of weapon.

View from inside tree stand blind. White plastic barrel (center of photo) is located 32 yds away. Additional white plastic barrel at bottom of screen (crushed by grizz) is set at 18 yds for bow shot.

Typical plastic barrel ratcheted a few feet off the ground due to sloping terrain. Note secondary container in tree (top left) for added scent. Photo courtesy of Bill Comer, Valdez, AK.

Time to fill your barrels with bait

Depending on where you live will determine which types of bait are the most economical for you. Since I live 12 hours round trip from the nearest big box store, I tend to stock up on cheap Walmart dog food in 55 lb bags whenever I am in Anchorage, Alaska throughout late winter and early spring each year—depending on how many trips I need to make for other business. Since my sons and I typically operate anywhere from 2 to 4 bait stations per season, we tend to go through—on average—1000 lbs of dog food per bear bait season. In addition to dog food, I start collecting leftover popcorn from the local movie theater in January or February as well as used fry grease from the local Chinese restaurant, starting in February or March. Also, I purchase scent baits from Bait Em 907 and Cabelas, far in advance of the April 15 season opener in my preferred GMU.

Be creative in your thinking. Some grocery stores will allow you to rummage through their dumpsters for expired bread, pastries, doughnuts, frosting canisters, etc. Look for sales on fruit jello mixes (non-citrus), confectioner sugar, pancake syrup, honey, molasses, and the like. Remember, bears live in a world of scents. The stronger the scent at your bait station, the faster you will attract and retain bears.

The skinned carcasses of furbearers and fur animals, as well as the meat from small game (excluding birds), may be used as bait. Additionally, the skin, guts, heads, or bones of game legally taken or road kill; and brown/grizzly bear meat and black bear meat (taken between June 1st and December 31st) are also viable bait sources. If fish is used—much like game—only the head, bones, guts, and skin may be used. Check the requirements in your specific GMU first.

A sample barrel setup may consist of the following:

1. Standing 55-gallon steel barrel chained to a tree with approximately 8-inch diameter hole in the upper ⅓ and small 1 inch holes spaced out along the bottom portion for scent/grease/food run-out
2. 2 (55lb) bags of inexpensive dog food (the cheaper the better)
3. 2 (5gal) containers of used fry oil from a local restaurant poured over the dog food

Additionally, I like to use a second plastic 50-gallon barrel lying on its side with an opening at one end. This is chained to the same tree through an opening in the opposite end. I then fill this barrel with as much leftover movie theatre popcorn as I have available and several containers of the cheapest pancake syrup I can find—and then lay it back on its side. This keeps the bears busy for some time and allows for longer lapses in bait checks for those of us that have to travel a bit farther to our selected locations.

What bait foods you use may depend on what bears you are baiting. If you're in an area where you can legally bait brown/grizzlies, then you may use less sweet-based foods and use more grease, meat or fish. If you are hunting predominantly black bears, then you may use sweeter-based baits (i.e. confectioner sugar, strawberry jello powder, syrup, etc.). Regardless—if you are focused on black bears and there are brown bears in the area, guess what…. You will eventually have brown bears at your bait site. In the end, use what you have or what is most readily available and go from there.

If you have the time and some minimal resources, you can experiment with making your own baits or "bear candy." For those of us that are overly anxious to start bear baiting—or simply experiencing cabin fever—creating simple lures out of marshmallows, corn syrup, jello-mix, and popcorn—can be a fun activity for the whole family. I have included one of my favorite bear bait recipes in the back, but you can find all kinds of creative mixes online via Youtube or other favorite internet sources.

Three popcorn "balls" made of popcorn, marshmallows, corn syrup, water & strawberry jello. They are held w/in an old tomato cage that had been modified & clipped to the chain. Lasted longer than I was anticipating—but would recommend putting them in your top-loading barrel as they are typically too large for a bear to pull thru the side hole.

50-gallon plastic barrel & 5-gallon bucket ratcheted/chained to tree—filled w/popcorn & used fry oil. The red square on top is a thin piece of metal attached w/hinges drilled directly thru the plastic. This allows the bait to be poured thru the top for faster refills.

As you can probably surmise by now, there is an infinite number of setups and bait-mixes you can use to establish your site. Do what works best for you without killing yourself physically (or financially) in the process.

Now what

Once you've set your stand and secured your barrels, the next step is to alter the area to assist you with shot placement. Use fallen limbs, large branches and/or small tree trunks to create a barricade or enclosure behind your barrel.

This will keep bears from approaching from behind the barrels and remaining obstructed from full view. By creating a backdrop, your bears will be "herded" towards the front of the barrel for better observation to determine size, sex and condition of their hides.

Once your site is set, place a game camera (or 2 if possible but not required) in close proximity to your barrel to capture images in your absence. Cameras should be set prior to handling baits, as curious bears will be drawn to your camera and the scent of food on the camera is a sure way to have your camera knocked out of position. As previously noted, cameras provide

33

critical hunting information including; times bears arrive and depart your station, what types of bears frequent your bait, the size of bears visiting your bait and the sex of the bears visiting your bait. Cameras also capture unexpected visitors you would otherwise miss, such as eagles, ravens, wolverines, porcupines, moose, ermine, marten, coyote and wolf, to name just a few.

Lastly, prior to departing the site, I always place a few large branches in the opening of my barrels. Though I have cameras, the branches give me an immediate notification when I return to my bait, as to whether I've had bears at the barrel. If the sticks are on the ground when I return, I know I've had bears at the bait and it's time to check the cameras. If the sticks are undisturbed, it tells me there's no sense wasting time checking cameras and sitting the stand—simple as that.

PART 5. JUDGING BEARS

AS PREVIOUSLY MENTIONED IN PART 1, judging the age, size, and sex of bears is extremely difficult at times—even to the most seasoned bear hunters. Bears are notoriously difficult to gauge due to a host of varying factors. Black bears don't reach full adult weight until they are 7-9 years old. Until then, male and female bears may look very similar in appearance.

Without the aid of trail camera photos, one might mistake this sow for a young boar—especially when she first arrived without her cubs.

The following is only a partial list to assist in the identification process:

Adult (Black Bear) Male (Boar) Characteristics:
a. **Head and Neck:**
   i. Wide square head and face
   ii. Ears appear small compared to rest of head and are set wide apart
   iii. Thick, blocky muzzle
   iv. Muscles bulge on the forehead creating a crease on large adult males

b. **Body size and Shape:**
   i. Large shoulders wider than head
   ii. Legs appear thick all the way down through thick ankles

c. **Urination:**
   i. Urinates straight down or forward

Adult (Black Bear) Female (Sow) Characteristics:
a. **Head and Neck:**
   i. Smallish, narrow head
   ii. Ears appear a bit larger as compared to rest of head but are closer together
   iii. Tapered muzzle (think German Shepherd or Collie)

b. **Body size and Shape:**
   i. Narrow shoulders approximately same width as head
   ii. Legs appear shorter, thinner and more tapered than males

c. **Urination:**
   i. Urinates towards the rear

Determining Age

Determining the exact age of a bear is impossible to do, despite the many hunters I have encountered over the years who merely open the mouth of a dead bear and—based on the look of its teeth—throw out a random age. The only true way to determine age is to pull a tooth and examine the number of rings under a microscope. A black bear is considered an adult at around five years old, though bears have been known to live well into their thirties.

Young Female: note narrow elongated face.

Approximate determinations are based on size, shape, and demeanor. Oddly enough, attitude can often determine if a bear is an older trophy-worthy specimen. Older bears are more confident and often enter your bait site with less hesitation than younger bears.

Mature Male: note broad head/neck.

Important Note: You may **NOT** (in the vast majority of GMUs) take a cub or a sow accompanied by cubs. This should go without saying, but unfortunately, there are always those that conduct themselves in a less-than-ethical manner.

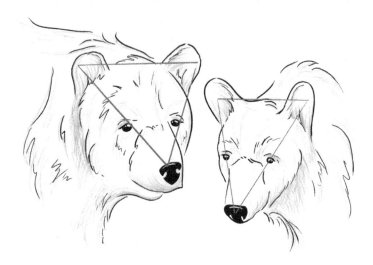

Note: larger/older bears have a wider head while younger bears have a narrow head/face.

Determining species

It is important to do your research in advance and familiarize yourself with the differences between black bears and grizzly bears (also referred to as brown bears when located within the coastal ranges of Alaska). Depending on which GMU you are hunting in will determine which bears will be most prevalent at your bait site. Bait sites that are frequented predominantly by brown/grizzly bears, will most likely see limited black bears, though this is merely a generalization—again—based on the individual GMU(s) you choose to hunt. Don't hesitate to seek out advice from experienced hunters and trappers who may be more familiar with a specific area. Just keep in mind, sometimes you get what you "pay for" and free advice isn't always worth its value. For example, I once decided to set up a site in an area

I was unfamiliar with and sought input from several "seasoned" hunters regarding the likelihood of bringing bears to a particular area of the mountain. I was told again and again that there were no black bears in the area due to the high number of brown/grizzly bears that frequented this particular region. Since this GMU allowed the taking of both black and brown bears over bait, I decided to set my sights on bringing in a large brown bear, and baited accordingly. After weeks of baiting and hundreds of trail camera pictures of black bears, my son was able to take one of the most beautiful cinnamon colored black bears we had ever seen. Yet, not a single brown/grizzly bear ever visited our site.

To start:

1. **Black bears** come in many different colors including; black, brown, cinnamon, bluish-black (glacier bears) and even white.

2. **Brown (or grizzly) bears** come in several different colors as well including; black, brown, blonde and a variation of one or more of these colors.

3. Although brown bears are typically larger than black bears, this alone is not a definitive factor in discerning between the two.

4. The best indicators (though not all-inclusive) include:
   a) Brown/Grizzly bears have larger shoulders than black bears
   b) Brown/Grizzly bears have a pronounced shoulder hump
   c) Brown/Grizzly bears have a concave (or dished) facial profile
   d) Brown/Grizzly bears have much larger claws than black bears

This large Black Bear (Boar) squared at 6 ft.

Mother and cub. "Cinnamon" colored Black Bears visiting bait site.

Brown/Grizzly Bear cubs at same site.

First Black Bear (Boar) of Spring Season: Squared at 6ft.

"Blonde" Brown/Grizzly Bear visiting what is predominantly
a Black Bear Bait Site.

Monster Brown/Grizzly Bear tearing down beaver carcass.
Beaver was placed at height of 12 ft.

Eagle vs. Black Bear. If a bear battles an eagle in the woods,
and no one's there to see it—did it really happen?

PART 6. SHOT PLACEMENT

Bow vs. Gun

REGARDLESS OF THE WEAPON(S) YOU CHOOSE, nothing is more important than taking the time to practice your shooting skills **BEFORE** you head out to the field. This will help ensure your guns and/or bows are properly sighted-in as well as bolstering your confidence while making that adrenaline-filled shot. Know your maximum effective range while trying—as realistically as possible—to simulate shooting conditions and scenarios you will face from your stand. For example: If you are planning to shoot from your stand in a heavy parka and gloves, then make sure you practice shooting outfitted this same way. If you are shooting from a tree stand eighteen (18) ft high at the shooting rail, then practice shooting from an elevated location. If you're using your bow and you need to shoot from a sitting position because the canopy on your stand won't allow you to stand up straight, then practice your shots while sitting. You get the point—right? Remember...the first time you try to make a challenging (perhaps out of the ordinary) shot should NOT be while shooting at a live animal.

One unique aspect of bear physiology is the fact that bears have very large circulatory systems. The main difference between a human's circulatory system and a bear's is that bears have far

43

more (and larger) veins and valves. As a result, this tends to hasten the loss of blood when struck in a vital location. This, combined with a bear's large respiratory system (large lung capacity) allows for a rather generous area for effective shot placement.

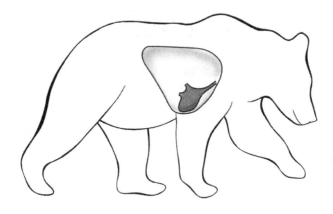

Based on these factors, a broadside shot is preferred whenever possible. The saying for bears is to aim for "the middle of the middle" meaning the center mass behind the front shoulder. Always wait for him to extend his near foreleg *forward* before taking your shot. This provides an open path to the heart and forward lung area rather than striking the front shoulder first.

By planning ahead and visualizing your set-up, you can influence the positioning of bears at your site. For example: If you place your barrel with the front opening facing towards your stand, the bears will generally position themselves facing (or angled) away from you as they feed at the barrel. If you place your barrel with the front opening facing off to the side while looking from your stand, the bears will generally position themselves broadside to you as they feed at the barrel. Keep in mind: regardless of positioning—over time—food and scent will eventually be spread around your site providing the bears with many "interesting" spots to explore and forage.

Note: bait barrels positioned to lay on their sides will be rolled back and forth on a regular basis as the bears reach in to extract food. Don't forget to reposition your barrel to provide for your preferred shot angle, **prior to** climbing into your stand for the day/night.

However, despite these efforts, you will often be faced with a shot that has your bear angled (or quartered) either towards, away or straight on. In these cases, it is important to visualize the path of your bullet or arrow before you shoot. I find that shot placement using a broadhead is more forgiving than when using a 30-06 round...though my 45-70 has seemed to help compensate for that aspect of my shooting :)

1. With a bear quartering **toward** you, your target should be somewhere between the base of the neck and the point of the front shoulder facing you.

2. With a bear quartering **away**, your target should be such that the bullet will enter far enough behind the near side shoulder so that it will pass through and break the far side shoulder (the one you can't see). Be careful not to shoot too far back or you will end up "gut" shooting your bear—which will eventually kill your bear—undoubtedly far from where he can easily be located.

3. With a bear facing **directly at you,** you want to aim for the center of the base of its neck as its head is lowered while feeding.

4. I personally **do not recommend** shooting at a bear when he is facing **directly away from you.** There are just too many obstacles on your bullet's or arrow's trajectory to ensure a quick, ethical kill. There are

undoubtedly many who would disagree with this statement, so I say, "to each, his own." The choice lies with the hunter.

With that said, I have personally observed black bears traveling easily over 100 yards through thick undergrowth after having been shot through the heart or both lungs. On another occasion, I observed an 8 ft brown/grizzly bear travel only a few yards before dropping after being struck by a single arrow. In the end, each bear is different and should be respected for its strength, courage, and desire to survive. Fatally wounded bears generally operate on 100% adrenaline and should be dealt with cautiously. Especially when still in the "recovery" phase following your shot, as you wind your way through thick stands of alders and brush that inherently limit the effectiveness of long rifles or bows.

In the end, shot placement is about patience, precision, and compassion. It is our duty—as stewards of nature's resources—to ensure we dispatch our bear as efficiently and painlessly as possible. Be mindful of this moment and respect the animal... before, during and after.

Note: When hunting bears with:

Bow and Arrow. The minimum peak draw weight for:

1. Black bears is 40 pounds
2. Brown/Grizzly bears is 50 pounds
3. Arrows must be a minimum of 20 inches in overall length, tipped with a non-barbed broadhead, and at least 300 grains in total weight.
4. An ADF&G-approved Bowhunter Certification Course is required to hunt big game with a bow if born on or after January 1st, 1986 in certain GMUs. This must be carried with you in the field.

Crossbow. The minimum peak draw weight must be—regardless of species—at least 100 pounds. The bolt must be at least 16 inches in overall length, tipped with a non-barbed broadhead and at least 300 grains in total weight.

1. You must complete an ADF&G-approved Crossbow Certification Course, regardless of GMU or age of the hunter.

Muzzleloader. You may not hunt big game with a muzzleloader unless you have successfully completed an ADF&G approved muzzleloader hunter education course that includes ballistic limitations of muzzleloading weapons and a proficiency test.

General Gun Choice. The question of all questions, that has been asked a million times, right? What gun is best for bears? The answer is simple…it depends! Many people believe the bigger the better and, to some extent, I agree. If I'm hunting brown/grizzly bears, then the more stopping power, the better. I would rather not have to go on an extended mile-long "explore" through thick brush and alders to find my downed bear. It is much less "exciting" to climb down out of your blind after having observed your bear go down (and relinquish his death moan), then to see him "disappear" in thick brush and go silent. This is not to say that you have to replace your trusty 30-06 if you want to hunt anything other than black bears. This is simply providing one point of view.

There is much to be said about using a gun that you are both comfortable and proficient with, as shot placement is just as (if not more) important as caliber. However, for those folks who don't want to purchase more than two or three guns (I'm not sure who these people are but I'm told they do exist), then you should be focusing on versatility, or to put it in more basic terms;

what else are you planning to hunt with this gun? Other factors include basic hunting preferences such as: do you typically hunt with friends and/or family members or do you typically hunt alone. Do you carry a sidearm (pistol or revolver) for back-up or close-quarter situations, such as slogging through thick stands of alders which would render your long gun ineffective?

For example: in the past, I have always hunted with my sons. As such, we would have scouted out individual bears using trail camera footage and decided in advance, who was hunting that day. The other person or persons then acted as back-up. Typical gun distribution usually looked something like this:

a. The primary hunter would carry a scoped 30-06 (along with a 45 caliber pistol).
   i. The secondary would carry a 12 gauge shotgun loaded with bear slugs (along with a 40 caliber pistol or 460 magnum revolver).
b. If the primary hunter is bow hunting, then they would carry just their sidearm.
   i. The secondary would carry a 12 gauge shotgun or 45-70.

However, now that my sons are older and have lives of their own, they're not always available to hunt whenever that big boar shows up on camera, so I've taken to hunting solo on occasion. In these cases, I revert to using my Henry 45-70 with iron sights, along with my 45 caliber pistol. I will say that when hunting alone, it is extremely advantageous to drop your bear as close to the barrel as possible, for many obvious reasons. On my most recent solo excursion, I took a 6ft squared black bear with my Henry (while filming) and was fortunate enough to recover him less than 20 yards from the barrel. Of course, regardless of caliber, shot placement is key!

So, what guns are popular with Alaskan Bear Baiters? Though the answers are as varied as the hunters themselves, here is a sample list of favorites. Please remember that this is not intended to be all-inclusive, or even close to representing a comprehensive review or endorsement:

- .270 Winchester
- .308 Winchester
- .30-06 (many believe this is the best all-around gun for AK hunting)
- Marlin 1895 (.450 Marlin)
- Henry .45-70 Government
- Remington Model 700 (.375)
- Remington 870 (12 gauge)
- Ruger Hawkeye Alaska (.375 Ruger)
- Winchester Model 70 Alaskan (.375 H&H)

In the end, and the common thread that runs throughout this book, is to do what works best for you and your particular hunting style or methods. Do your homework and research the web, speak with other hunters, and above all else, start putting a little extra money aside each month so you can afford that new gun safe. Remember, you ALWAYS need more room than you think you do!

PART 7. AFTER THE SHOT

ALL THE LONG DAYS, WEEKS AND MONTHS of hard work, preparation and patience have finally paid off and you have been fortunate enough to take a shot at a bear of your choosing. Now what?

1. Can you confirm you hit your mark? Many a hunter has let the excitement of the moment hurry their shot and shoot high, low or somewhere unknown. How did the bear react? Did he rear-up, spin around, roll forward/backward, roar out…or simply run away? Sometimes it's unquestionable, sometimes it's not.

2. For those who video their hunts, the ability to playback the moment of the shot can prove invaluable. Slowing down the footage can capture the bear's immediate reaction and help confirm both whether the bear was hit and just as important, where it was hit. A shot placed too far back or too high may not prove lethal and will undoubtedly lead to an exciting time in the bush figuring out the answer to that question.

3. Once your shot has been fired—regardless of your weapon of choice—do your best to keep your eyes on your bear until; 1) he has dropped or; 2) he is no longer visible due to terrain or other factors.

4. This is the time to exercise additional patience and remain as quiet as possible—listening for any sounds, no matter how subtle. The sound of breaking branches, twigs, rattling bushes or rushing leaves all may indicate the movement of an injured bear in heavy brush.

5. Patience in the stand *following* the shot is just as important as patience in the stand *prior* to the shot. Ideally, you want to wait until you hear what is referred to as "the death moan." This is the bear's last exclamation of life and typically indicates the bear is down, and the end is near. Though an assuring sound to most hunters, not all bears will herald the arrival of their own demise. For these bears, additional caution is needed prior to leaving your stand and venturing in pursuit of your prey. Many hunters—including myself—have waited for what we assume to be a suitable amount of time (20-30 minutes) only to realize the bear is still conscious and aware, which typically leads to driving the bear deeper into the brush as he slowly succumbs to his wounds. Each year, there are stories of just the opposite scenario occurring…hunters head into the woods to "recover" their bear only to realize the bear is far from dead. At this point, it's a virtual coin-toss as to which side of the bear's instinctive "fight" or "flight" side will land in your favor. If in doubt, stay in your stand until the adrenaline of taking your shot wears off, your

hands stop shaking and you feel comfortable under the current conditions. Unless you're absolutely sure your bear is down, tracking a potentially wounded bear is not a recommended solo activity.

Tracking

An important point to remember when setting out to look for your bear is to keep in mind the traditional or predominant direction the bears travel to and from your bait site. Bears typically establish set patterns of behavior and use and reuse the same set of trails as they make their way across their accustomed hunting grounds. This is an important factor, as a wounded bear will be operating on pure adrenaline and basic survival instinct which often drives him—consciously or unconsciously—back from which he came. This will often assist in your tracking efforts if you are having difficulty determining which direction your bear has gone. The following may prove useful:

1. Ensure you always carry **survey tape** (bright orange/pink, etc.) in your pack to mark blood sign. This can be purchased at any hardware store or home improvement center.

2. Immediately start from the spot the bear was sitting/standing when first shot and attempt to locate blood sign. As many bears are taken in the waning light of an Alaskan summer evening, it may become difficult to see blood signs when the sun has dropped below the mountain tops and the shadows overtake the landscape. Tie a small piece of survey tape to mark the first sign of blood.

3. If it becomes too dark to safely track your bear, stop, back out and return first thing in the morning.

4. Continue to scan the ground and surrounding bushes for blood while your partner keeps their head up and ready to respond to the possibility of a charging bear. Continue to mark blood spots/smears or splatters with surveyor tape. At times, the blood may be very pronounced and at other times, blood splatter may be subtle or non-existent. It all depends on the bear and the shot placement.

5. If the trail goes cold, don't hesitate to re-start from the beginning. Try to visualize where a wounded bear would go given your particular bait site and hunting terrain. It's important not to give up and if necessary, call in some help, to get more "eyes on" as a few more people may make all the difference between locating and losing your bear.

6. Once your bear is located, approach cautiously and be prepared—if necessary—to discharge your weapon. Never walk-up on a downed bear without your weapon and/or your partner's weapon trained on him.

7. **Lastly: Don't forget to mark/notch your harvest ticket with the day/month of your kill.**

Keep in mind: While you may use a motorized vehicle to locate your bear, you may NOT use a motorized vehicle to pursue a bear that is fleeing.

Congratulations!!! All your hard work has paid off and you have successfully harvested a bear. **NOW** the real work begins! Time to decide your next move. Do you field dress your bear "in place" or can you manage to transport him out of the field and back to a more controllable environment.

This decision usually depends on a number of factors, including; the size of the bear, terrain in which he died, and the weather (including the predominance of mosquitos), to name a few. In my experience, bears rarely die in a convenient location. As previously mentioned, once injured, bears tend to instinctively navigate from whence they came—meaning thick alders, high grasslands or steep terrain marked with numerous deadfalls and other obstacles. Add to this the fact that you have been baiting your site for weeks (or months) and this bear is not the only bear that has been regularly frequenting your bait site. There are few things more distracting than trying to skin out a bear in limited visibility while other bears are wandering all around you as they try to get to your barrel—especially if that bear is a momma bear with cubs! More times than not, at a minimum, you will have to drag your bear to some open area or create an opening with your tree saw in order to lay out your tarp and stretch out your bear. This is where the value of a hard plastic sled really makes its mark. Again, If the terrain allows, you can load a good size bear into your sled and drag it out to an open location (or to your 4-wheeler) and decide from there.

55

If you are on a multiple-day hunt, far from home or your bear is just too large to extract from the field, then field dressing is your best bet. If you're within an hour or two of home—as the majority of bear bait stations are located—then you may have the option of hauling him out, loading him up and unloading him in the driveway or garage for a more comfortable salvage job. The choice is up to you.

Remember: The hides of ALL Brown/Grizzly Bears and of Black Bears taken in certain GMUs, MUST have proof of sex naturally attached to the hide or meat until sealing requirements have been met.

And certainly don't forget the **Photo Op**! Whether you decide to capture the moment with or without a weapon in hand, always remember to be respectful of the animal and its surroundings. As hunters and conservationists, we have an inherent responsibility, whenever possible, to showcase our passion for hunting and the great outdoors, in a respectful manner suitable for social media and/or public scrutiny.

Despite our best efforts, there will always be those who question hunting. Take the time to educate yourself so you, in turn, can educate the "politically correct" public on the tangible value hunting provides by contributing towards habitat conservation and restoration. And most importantly, encourage and inspire the next generation of young hunters to carry on this essential lifestyle.

PART 8. SKINNING AND SALVAGE

AS ALWAYS, IT'S IMPORTANT TO CHECK the current hunting regulations for your particular GMU to determine what you are required to salvage in way of meat and/or hide. Requirements vary depending on the unit, time of year (either January 1st thru May 31st or June 1st thru December 31st), and species you are harvesting. From a personal perspective, we have a simple family rule: you eat what you kill. Bear—whether black or brown/grizzly—makes great eating if prepared properly.

Generally speaking—the following applies regardless of GMU:

Salvage for Black Bears:

1. In all areas of Alaska from *January 1st to May 31st,* **edible meat** must be salvaged and removed from the field. ADF&G defines "edible meat" as:
   a. Meat from the front quarters
   b. Meat from the hindquarters
   c. Meat along the backbone (backstraps and tenderloins)

2. This meat may NOT be used for pet food or bait.

3. The hide and skull may not be transported from the field until the edible meat has been salvaged.

4. You may use the carcass of a skinned black bear taken June 1st to December 31st, as animal food or bait as long as the hide is salvaged.

Salvage for Brown/Grizzly Bears:

1. You must salvage the entire hide (with claws attached) and skull—unless it was taken in (and not removed from) one of the subsistence hunt areas under a subsistence registration permit. Check the hunting regulations under "Brown/grizzly bear subsistence hunting."

2. When taken under a subsistence permit, in addition to the meat termed "edible," you must also salvage all of the meat of the neck, brisket, and ribs.

3. You may use the carcass of a skinned brown/grizzly bear as animal food or bait as long as it does not conflict with subsistence regulations.

For either species—you are not required to salvage the meat of the head, guts, bones, sinew, and meat left on the bones after trimming. You're also not required to salvage meat that's been damaged and made inedible by the bullet or arrow (such as a shoulder shot which destroys a large portion of the front quarter). These parts can be left in the field because they're not included in the definition of "edible meat."

As previously noted, it is not the intent of this publication to replace or circumvent the most current edition of the Alaska hunting regulations. To ensure full compliance, familiarize yourself with all applicable salvage requirements before harvesting your bear.

Skinning: Rug vs. Full/Shoulder Mount.

Whether skinning your 1st bear or your 50th bear, you should have some idea as to what you will do with the hide **BEFORE** you make your first cut.

Bears skinned out for rugs or hangers.
Photo courtesy of Bill Comer, Valdez, AK.

There are numerous videos online to assist you with skinning out your bear. In addition and if possible, speak with your local taxidermist for advice and guidance. The fewer mistakes you make in the field will result in fewer mistakes to be fixed in the taxidermist's shop—making their job that much easier and reducing unnecessary costs in modifications or repairs to your hide. Though obviously dependent on where you live and what resources are available to you—I have personally asked our local taxidermist to meet with a group of hunters at the local museum (large hunting stores may serve the same purpose) and demonstrate some preferred methods (from beginning to end) on an existing mount. If this is not an option, try reaching out to other fellow hunters and ask if you can observe and/or assist in skinning out their animal. Though certainly not technical in nature, skinning out your first bear can be a bit intimidating, so take your time and don't be afraid to ask for help when needed.

So, in the most general terms possible, consider the following:

If planning to make a rug or "hanger" (just the tanned bear hide itself): roll your bear over on its back and cut from throat to tail down the center of its belly (keeping evidence of sex attached to the hide). Then from the center of the inside paws to the chest where it meets up with your center cut—then skin from the belly outwards to the sides and back—and eventually up to the neck where you can sever the head from the hide.

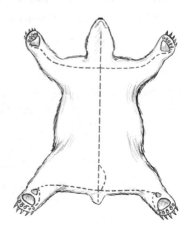

If planning a full or shoulder mount: start your cut from the back of the neck and cut down the spine and through the hide to the tail and skin from the back outward to the sides and belly. I always find this method most intimidating as you're cutting through the best part of the hide.

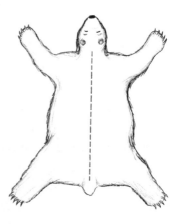

Note: On either method, always cut with your blade "up" thru the hide so you're not cutting down thru the hair (and dulling your knife at the same time).

Skinning a black bear for a rug. Note paws removed from torso and left in
hide along with head. Photo courtesy of Bill Comer, Valdez, AK.

Skinned out on gravel beach.
Photo courtesy of Bill Comer, Valdez, AK.

For detailed drawings, videos, and information that will
actually be useful, go to **www.adfg.alaska.gov** and search for
specific information pertaining to harvesting bears or search
online under videos for "how to skin a bear."

Remember: The hides of ALL Brown/Grizzly Bears and of Black Bears taken in certain GMUs, MUST have proof of sex naturally attached to the hide or meat until sealing requirements have been met. Nothing is more helpful than actually seeing it done—at least for us "visual learners."

PART 9. SEALING REQUIREMENTS

1. All <u>Brown/Grizzly Bears</u> **MUST** be sealed, regardless of which GMU it was harvested from.

2. <u>Black Bears</u> taken in certain GMUs must be sealed (check the ADF&G regulations for specific exemptions).

3. Sealing must be completed within 30 days of the kill, or less as required by whatever permit you hold.

WHAT DOES THE TERM *SEALING* mean? According to ADF&G, the term *"sealing"* is defined as taking the skull and/or hide (with claws and proof of sex attached) of the bear you killed, to an officially designated "sealing officer." Typically your local taxidermist or a Wildlife Trooper can assist you in this process.

See the "Important Information for all bear hunters" section of the Alaska Hunting Regulations under "Sealing Requirements" for additional information on the sealing process.

PART 10. POST-SEASON SITE CLEAN-UP

AFTER MONTHS OF PREPARATION and hard work, including countless hours in the stand, the end of the season is often bittersweet. As often as not, the last thing you feel like doing after a successful—or not so successful—bear baiting season, is site clean-up. However, as both hunters and conservationists, this step in the annual process is essential to maintaining a sustainable program. I have personally been culpable for failing to perform site cleanup in a timely manner and have been cited accordingly by the Troopers. In order to head off future problems, the following guidelines apply:

1. All bait, litter, and equipment must be removed from the bait site when hunting is completed. This includes all lures and attractants.
   a. In my case, the season ended at midnight on June 30th and I had not yet removed my empty barrel when the new Trooper visited my site on July 4th.
   b. Depending on the remoteness of your site—work and travel schedules may preclude you from getting to your site for final cleanup in a timely manner. Many of us face this same challenge each season and choose to roll the dice and remediate

our sites as soon as reasonably possible following the end of the season. It is best to select your own end-of-season date **prior to** the official closure, in order to afford you the time necessary to do a thorough cleanup. If not, you have no one to blame but yourself.

2. ADF&G defines *"equipment"* as; barrels, tree stands/blinds, game cameras, and other items associated with your bear bait station.
   a. Tree stands may be left in the field year-round provided you obtain permission from the landowner or other organization or entity authorized to give permission. You may want to obtain this permission in advance if you are planning to build your own stand as removing these can be a real "pain in the butt." Again…I speak from experience when saying this!

3. Cleaning up and restoring your bait site to pre-season conditions is extremely important as the end-results can either promote or detract from the public's support of bear baiting operations. Ensure all "parts and pieces" are collected from the surrounding areas—*including that plastic grease container that the bears have inevitably torn into 100 pieces and strewn throughout the woods.* Bottom Line: Carry Out what you Carried In!

PART 11. MISCELLANEOUS INFO

A. Hunting in the rain

I HAVE HEARD THIS QUESTION asked many times over the years, having asked it myself from time to time; do bears visit bait sites in the rain? The simple answer is "sometimes." I have seen many a hunter on social media stating that they took their biggest bears in the rain, while others have stated they have never been successful in the rain. From simple observation, I have viewed many bears via trail camera pictures, visiting my sites in the rain. My in-person experiences vary slightly. The reality is I have seen bears at our sites during times **just before** and **shortly after** large bands of rain, but generally speaking, I have seen far fewer bears in the rain than not.

The other more apparent reason for this is simply the fact that I hate bear hunting in the rain, therefore I tend to limit my hours in the stand to more favorable weather conditions. For some, time is limited and you have to hunt while/when you can. Regardless of when you hunt, try to keep in mind a bad (or wet) day of bear hunting is far better than a good day at the office. As bear baiters, we are literally living thousands of people's bucket lists of lifetime adventures—we just get to do it again and again.

B. Choosing the right trail camera

Another topic with lots of opinions, so here's mine: you don't need to spend $100s of dollars on elaborate trail cameras to be successful. I typically buy cameras ONLY when on sale and I try never to spend more than $60-70 per camera. The one exception I made was a remote/wireless camera that sent photos to my cell phone from my bait site located over 90 miles from my house. It cost over $400 and was fantastic…when it worked as designed. I'm not saying there is anything wrong with buying the latest/greatest game camera technology. If you want to and you have some extra money to spend—good for you. I'm merely stating that your average mid-range trail camera will suffice for what you really need it for. And what is that you ask? Simply put:

1. I *need* to see how big the bears are in comparison to some reference point (my barrel) in the photo
2. I *need* to adequately identify which bears are juveniles, females and males
3. I *need* to see bears in the dark
4. I *like* at times to capture video—more for entertainment purposes than a need to get the info in items 1 thru 3 above
5. And I *need* the pictures to be time-stamped so I can figure out any recurring patterns

Please Be Aware: As of the *2018-2019 Regulatory Year*—the use of live/wireless cameras to aid in the take of game is prohibited in Alaska. This also includes airborne, remote-controlled cameras or videos (drones). In addition to the rule for wireless cameras, a second part of the rule covers other "wireless communication" devices (such as cell phones and satellite phones). The rule prohibits taking game with the aid of these other "wireless communication" devices until 3 a.m. on the day after these devices are used (the same as if you flew and hunted the same day). From a personal perspective, this confuses the issue even more due to the fact that in many GMUs, bears may be taken at a bait station the same day you have flown (see below). Consult your Wildlife Trooper for further clarification and hopefully, the Board of Game will continue to refine this aspect of the regulations as technology becomes more prevalent over time.

That's it. What I have come to learn over the years is that it is wise (and often needed) to have more than one camera at your bait site. Whether bears knock down your camera, trespassers mess with your equipment, or Troopers visit in your absence, an additional camera (or 2) sometimes makes all the difference. So, do the math and decide for yourself, but don't get caught up in the "latest and greatest"...unless you want to.

C. Flying and Hunting the Same Day

Generally speaking, it is illegal to hunt or help someone else take big game **until** 3:00 a.m. the day following the day you have flown. **However**, in many GMUs, both black and brown bears may be taken at permitted bait stations the same day you have flown, as long as you are at least 300 feet from the airplane.

Keep in Mind: Same day airborne hunts are **NOT** allowed on National Park Service lands.

D. Squaring a Bear Hide

One of the first questions asked after hearing that you harvested a bear is "how big" was he? A fair enough question and one that you want to know as well. There are many ways to answer that question, but a good standard to use is by "squaring" your bear hide after skinning. The squared measurement of the hide is a good way to judge a bear's size and gives you a standard reference to compare "apples to apples" and "bears to bears."

The simple way to do this is: measure the width (tip of front paw to front paw with arms outstretched) and length (nose to tail). Add the two together, and then divide the total by two and you get the **squared size** of the bear. Black bears squaring 5-6 feet are about average. A bear over 6 feet is excellent, and seven-foot bears are monsters worthy of lifetime bragging rights.

When looking for an older bear that will square over 6 feet, make note of the position of its ears and their size. If the ears look small on a bear compared to the size of its head, it's likely a trophy animal. If they appear to grow out the side of the head, that also indicates a larger than average bear. If ears poke up on top of the bear's head and look large (think Mickey Mouse), chances are it has a few more years to go before becoming shot-worthy.

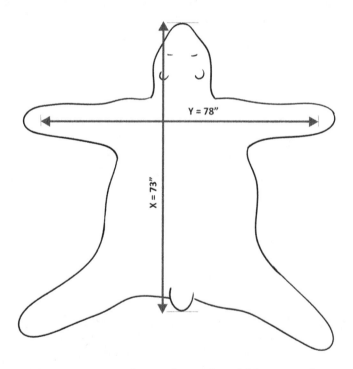

How to measure (square) your bear hide: Example

Length (tip of nose to tip of tail) = X,
Width (Front claw tip to claw tip) = Y,
let us assume X=73" and Y= 78"
X (73") + Y (78") /2 = Z (75.5")
or convert to squared feet Z (75.5") /12 = 6.292' (FT).

E. Regulatory Year Bag Limits

The reason I mention this is because I ran into a confusing situation (at least for me) while operating two different bait stations in two different GMUs with two different bag limits.

Specifically, I was operating a station in GMU 6D (which had a (1) black bear every regulatory year under a permit) while operating a second station in GMU 13D (which had a 3 black bear every regulatory year bag limit).

So, in "bear hunter math" how many bears could I actually take? Could I take a total of four bears: (3) bears in GMU 13 + (1) bear in GM 6 = 4 (right?). **WRONG!**

After asking several fellow hunters and getting several different answers, I went to the experts—you know, the ones who will issue the citation when I screw this up—the local Wildlife Trooper.

The answer was: since the largest bag limit in a single GMU was (3), that was the total number of black bears I could take in the regulatory year (July 1st—June 30th). However, I had to take the first bear in the GMU with the single bear bag limit first or lose my opportunity to take a bear in that unit. Then I could take the remaining (2) bears from my (3) bear total from the other unit.

If after reading this, I have confused you even more, please don't hesitate to contact your local Trooper for clarification. Believe me—they would rather take the time to educate you in advance rather than educate you via enforcement measures "after the fact"—and so would you!

F. Will a bear return once he's been shot at (and missed)?

The answer is "most likely" provided he has had time to acclimate to the bait site. If you check your cameras, and he's a regular, then my guess is: **he'll be back.** Three of the bears pictured in the back of this book (and below) were "misses" the first time around:

1. The first one was actually struck with a blunt "piece" of an arrow—and returned 5 minutes later to "make the book."

2. The second one was shot at and missed cleanly—only to have him end up on camera 4 days later and taken that same week.

3. The third one is a bit embarrassing, but here goes: The first time I tried hunting with a compound bow, I was shooting from a sitting position in my ladder stand, waiting for this bear to leave the main bait and work his way towards our secondary bait sitting 18 yds in front of me. After some time, we realized he wasn't coming in and I decided to take the long shot rather than wait for another opportunity. As a result, I managed to shoot clean over the bear, which only startled him a bit, but not enough to leave the bait. Thinking luck was with me, I knocked another arrow, but *"doing that thing my son always tells me I'm doing*

when I'm pulling back, and I say I'm not" my thumb inadvertently hit the arrow release, sending my 2nd arrow to that place where lost things go to hide. By this time, the bear had had enough of our shenanigans and bolted from the barrel—stopping briefly on the other side of a short bluff at the tree line to assess the situation. It was at this point I abandoned my archery ambitions and somehow thought it was now a good idea to grab my 45-70 and take a questionable shot at only a partial target. Suffice to say…I was pretty sure I had seen the last of that big boy. It's pretty bad when your "smartalek" son apologizes because he's out of weapons to hand you. Yet to my surprise, he was back on camera only days later, allowing my son to take him with his bow at 35 yds.

In the end, bears will do what bears will do. If you have a regular at your site, and he is spooked off for any number of reasons, he will most likely come back to your bait. The downside may be that he changes up his routine and goes nocturnal rather than showing up at those convenient mid-day meals.

Note distinctive scar on front shoulder that passes across chest and out opposite side. Remnants of a luckier day for this bear.

Another possible outcome, and one I've foolishly worried about over the years, is due to the ever-increasing hunting pressure throughout Alaska. Let's be honest, chances are your bear is cheating on you with another bear baiter in your area. Personal example: I was talking with a good friend of mine who had a bait station established nearly 11 miles from my site, and I had mentioned that we had spent over 40 hours scouting this very unique "red" colored black bear at our site, and my son had finally had an opportunity at him...and missed.

My friend then mentioned in passing that he also had a very distinctive "red bear" on camera at his bait, and had planned to go with his daughter this very evening and attempt to harvest him. At that point, I hesitantly asked the critical question, "did your bear happen to have a large, visible scar across his chest?" To which he answered "yes." At that point, the race was on! That night, we both headed for our sites, but as luck would have it, my son and I had Alaska's bipolar weather on our side for once. My friend ended up stopping by our trailhead on his way *back* home, just as we were loading up to head out to our stand. He and his daughter were drenched to the skin and chilled to the bone, after sitting through an isolated summer downpour, that targeted his remote portion of the valley. As a result, my son ended up taking "big red" two hours later.

Moral of the story: never share bear information specific to your bait station unless you're willing to let someone else benefit from your long hours of hard work and dedication.

PART 12. SIMPLE RECIPES
(For Bears & People)

For Bears: Marshmallow-Popcorn Ball

THIS IS ONE OF THE EASIER RECIPES, and one of my favorites—as the bears tend to love it and it's fairly inexpensive to make!

List of items/ingredients needed (remember, this is not an exact science):

1. (2) 5-Gallon buckets (ensure 1 bucket can fit inside the other)
2. Large cooking pot
3. Cooking spray
4. Plastic bag
5. Bucketful of old (or new) popcorn
6. 6-8 large bags of marshmallows
7. (2) to (4) 16oz bottles of corn syrup (light or dark)
8. (4) boxes of fruit flavored jello (strawberry, raspberry, etc.)—don't use citrus flavors
9. Vanilla extract
10. (4) cups water
11. A wife, husband, girlfriend, boyfriend or significant other, that will help clean up the mess you are about to make!

Preparation:
- Take (1) 5-gallon bucket and fill with popped popcorn
- Take a second 5-gallon bucket and **spray the entire insides with cooking spray**

STEP 1: Put all of your marshmallows in the cooking pot with 4 cups of water, and place on high heat. Keep stirring as the marshmallows become liquid.

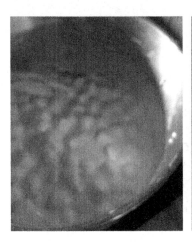
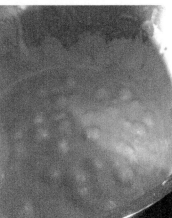

STEP 2: Keep stirring so the mixture won't burn to the bottom of your pot—add corn syrup, a small pour of vanilla, and powdered jello mix. Continue stirring mixture over high heat until all of your ingredients are well mixed and jello is dissolved. Remove from heat.

STEP 3: Pour about ¼ (or less) of dry popcorn into the bucket coated with cooking spray.

Dry popcorn in cooking spray-coated bucket.

STEP 4: Pour a small amount of your hot marshmallow mix over the popcorn and stir it up until the contents are coated.

STEP 5: Continue to repeat Steps 3 and 4 until your bucket is full and all of the popcorn is coated with your marshmallow mix.

STEP 6: Now, take your empty bucket (the one that originally held the popcorn) and place a plastic bag around its outside: the reason for this is because you are going to place this bucket inside the bucket with the popcorn mix (pushing it down into the bucket), keeping the two buckets from sticking together.

STEP 7: Now—push the empty bucket down HARD into the mix, compressing the marshmallow/popcorn mix. I typically stand in the empty bucket and hop up and down— usually next to something I can grab onto so I don't fall over and break my neck.

Mixing melted marshmallow mix into popcorn.

Standing in the dry bucket to compress mixture below.

77

STEP 8: Once compressed—remove the empty bucket (and plastic) and allow the compressed mix to sit for several hours—the longer you let it sit, the harder it will get. If you can wait until the next day—even better.

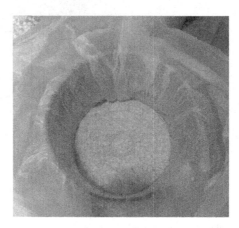

This is what it looks like after being compressed and the top bucket removed. Note: plastic was/is between the contents of the lower bucket and the empty bucket that was on top (the one we stood in).

STEP 9: Once set, turn the bucket upside down and gently bang the bottom and sides until the compressed popcorn ball comes out. Depending on how much cooking spray you used, it may come out easily or it may need some "love" from a rubber mallet (or similar object).

That's it—and you're done. Make as many as you want and keep them stored in a cool/dry space until you're ready to place them in your barrel or secure it to your bait station some other way. If placing in your barrel, you'll need a barrel with a removable lid, or an access hole that can accommodate the popcorn ball you just made. The point is to provide the bears with a distraction as they reach inside (along with your other barrel contents) and try to get at the "candy" center, without being able to pull the whole popcorn ball out of the barrel.

Feel free to experiment with the ingredients, as you can switch it up any way you like. I have chosen the least expensive set of ingredients, but you can substitute any number of sweetening agents for the corn syrup, including honey, molasses, pancake syrup, etc.

Oh…and those pots, pans, stirrers, and buckets don't get better with time—so get cleaning as soon after as possible—and have fun with it!

Color of popcorn balls varies depending on the type of jello-mix you add—this one is raspberry. These 4 popcorn balls were placed in an old tomato cage that was twisted into a "holder." I recommend placing them in your barrel or sturdier container as these didn't survive the first week, being chained to the outside of the barrel—live and learn.

For People: The World's Best Bear Stew

I make this stew quite often, and I have to say, it has converted more people to eating bear than any other method I have ever experienced. The appeal comes in the simplicity of the stew, resulting in a stew with absolutely zero game taste. Now, there are many who will consider this point as a detractor and I certainly understand…to each his own. But if you want a bear dish that appeals to a wide range of guests—both game and non-game lovers alike, then this is the dish for you.

What you'll need (again—not an exact science):

In advance: I suggest you marinade your bear meat ahead of time (preferably overnight) by:

1. Mixing 2-3 pounds of roughly cut meat with:
    a. ½ cup red wine vinegar
    b. ¼ cup oil (vegetable, canola or oil of choice)
    c. ⅛ to ¼ cup of McCormick's "Montreal Steak" seasoning. The more you use—the spicier the stew.

Once you're ready to get started, you'll need:

1. Crock Pot
2. 2-3 lbs of chunked or cubed marinated bear meat
3. 6-8 peeled carrots (chopped)
4. 6-peeled potatoes (chopped)
5. 4-stalks of celery (chopped)
6. 1-large sweet onion (chopped)
7. 1 generous tablespoon of beef-flavored "Better than Bullion" or similar-type beef bullion

(Optional items include: 1-bell pepper (I prefer red over green) & 1 teaspoon minced garlic)

STEP 1. Place chopped carrots, potatoes, celery, sweet onion (bell pepper & garlic if using) into crock pot. Then mix contents so vegetables are evenly distributed throughout.

STEP 2. Place marinated bear meat on top of vegetables, and distribute evenly OVER vegetables with spoon or spatula—do not mix meat into vegetables.

STEP 3. Mix 1 generous tablespoon of bullion into 1 to 1½ cups boiling water and mix until dissolved. Pour bullion mix evenly over meat in Crock Pot.

STEP 4. Cover pot and set on warm for 6-7 hours. After the first 2 to 3 hours, mix the meat and vegetables together until evenly distributed throughout—and re-cover. At this point, make sure the meat and vegetables are submerged below the liquid of the stew. Continue cooking.

STEP 5. That's all there is to it—enjoy! Pairs well with crescent rolls and your favorite beverage.

I personally enjoy having a framed photo of the bear we're eating (while he was alive) placed next to the pot as a tribute to his sacrifice, but I realize that's a bit weird, so feel free to roll your eyes and totally ignore this suggested act.

PART 13. PHOTOS

Youngest son's First Bear! After this "motley crew" scoured the mountain slopes (in the background) for what would later be confirmed as a "clean miss" we ran across this young Boar who was unwilling to vacate the bait site—snapping jaws and menacing moans alike.

First-time visitor to stand. This Boar waited at the tree line patiently, until we refilled the barrel. Then headed in before we even made it up the ladder.

This "cinnamon" colored black bear was initially struck by the knock of an arrow (the back end of an arrow) during a "you had to be there to believe it" arrow malfunction. He returned less than 5 minutes later a little more cautious but none the wiser.

This "cinnamon" colored black bear was taken in late May in remote, mountainous terrain in South Central.

Large black bear (Boar) squared at 6ft 3in.

This Boar was taken in mid-May and squared at 5ft 6in.

This Boar was taken on my first solo hunt in South Central Alaska using my
Henry 45-70—squaring at 6 ft even.

This "twin" Boar was taken in the same location as the bear above, just 1 week prior, and also squared at 6ft even.

The best side of "this guy" as we ferry barrels and bait ashore in Prince William Sound.

Large Prince William Sound Boar.
Photo courtesy of Bill Comer, Valdez, AK.

PART 14. HIDES

THERE ARE MANY OPTIONS WHEN it comes to finishing your bear hides. Rugs are a popular choice among many hunters, as they offer a variety of styles to choose from.

If choosing a "rug" style, think about whether you plan to actually place it on the floor or hang it on your wall. Different styles include mouth open/ears up, mouth open/ears down, mouth shut/ears up, mouth shut/ears down, snarled snout or smooth snout, etc., etc., etc.

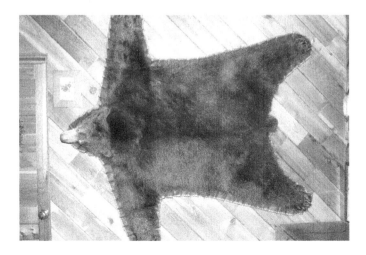

I have found that "ears back" rather than up, are best suited for actual floor rugs or on the walls of narrow hallways—otherwise they become a tripping hazard or have the potential to catch your shoulder as you walk by.

There is also the selection of felt background colors. Hint: Choosing a color closely matching the color of your bear will make your bears appear "fuller." Choosing a color lighter or darker than your bear will enhance the color of your bear.

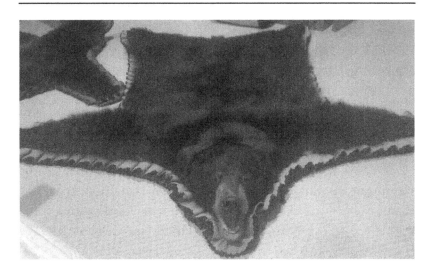

Rather than having a rug made, a simple "hanger" is often the easiest, fastest and most versatile way to display your bear. A hanger is just the tanned hide without a molded head or paws. These make a nice rustic display in any area of your home or office, and can be draped or hung.

Another *lesser* used method—but one I have come to REALLY like—is a method I came across after we harvested a brown/grizzly bear who had a beautiful head, but less than perfect hide. Rather than a rug or hanger, I chose to have our taxidermist tan the hide and then insert a molded head and paws. I then mounted the hide myself to an antique packboard that my wife bought me—simulating the look of hauling your bear out of the woods fresh from the hunt. In addition, it saves a significant amount of space as compared to a traditional rug, and can be easily hung like a painting. For others like me with limited wall space (think A-frame), this method is a welcome change from the ordinary.

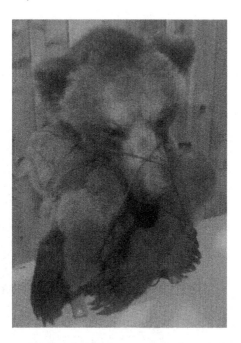

There are a host of other options, limited only by your imagination (and your checkbook). Additional choices include full body, shoulder mount, head mount, ¾ mounts, etc. Do what works best for you while honoring the memory of such a powerful, fearless predator.

About the Author

Thank you for reading my book, I hope you found it useful. Whether new to bear baiting or a seasoned bear hunter yourself, we all strive to constantly improve both our proficiency and efficiency as we engage in arguably—one of the most challenging and rewarding outdoor pursuits available to hunters today. I welcome your input and look forward to hearing from you @ bearbaitingak@gmail.com on your successes and lessons learned in the field. And never forget...as bear hunters, we are living a lifetime's worth of "bucket list" experiences each and every time we venture into the wilds of Alaska.

The author is a retired military officer who fell in love with Alaska the moment he and his family arrived on assignment, over a decade earlier.

Always the avid outdoorsman, he has successfully led fly-in caribou hunts on the North Slope, moose hunts in western Alaska, and spent nearly a month slogging loads up and down the Alaska Range while fulfilling his lifelong dream of climbing Denali. Despite these (and many more) "once in a lifetime" experiences in the Last Frontier, he considers bear baiting to be his one-true passion—anxiously awaiting each new bear season with the same excitement and optimism as the first.

Field Notes/Sketches

Field Notes/Sketches

Field Notes/Sketches

Field Notes/Sketches

Field Notes/Sketches

Field Notes/Sketches

Field Notes/Sketches

Field Notes/Sketches

Field Notes/Sketches

Field Notes/Sketches

DATE	TIME OF DAY	LOCATION	WEATHER/ TEMP	BEAR: TYPE/ SIZE/SEX

DATE	TIME OF DAY	LOCATION	WEATHER/ TEMP	BEAR: TYPE/ SIZE/SEX

First Bear = Lifetime of memories

Headed back to the truck after a long day of hauling equipment and bait. All-Terrain Vehicles prove invaluable when choosing remote baiting locations throughout Alaska.

Made in the USA
Monee, IL
30 May 2021